DATE DUE AR 4.9

JUL 2 1 2005			

Grace Hopper
Computer Whiz

Patricia J. Murphy

Enslow Publishers, Inc.

40 Industrial Road	PO Box 38
Box 398	Aldershot
Berkeley Heights, NJ 07922	Hants GU12 6BP
USA	UK

http://www.enslow.com

For my mother,
who has always inspired me to follow my dreams . . .
With love, P. J. M.

Library of Congress Cataloging-in-Publication Data

Murphy, Patricia J., 1963–
    Grace Hopper : computer whiz / Patricia J. Murphy.— 1st ed.
      p. cm. — (Famous inventors)
    Includes index.
    ISBN 0-7660-2273-0
    1. Hopper, Grace Murray—Juvenile literature. 2. Admirals—United States—BiographyJuvenile literature.
3. Computer engineers—United States—Biography—Juvenile literature. 4. United States. Navy—
Biography—Juvenile literature. 5. Inventors—United States—Biography—Juvenile literature. [1. Hopper,
Grace Murray. 2. Computer engineers. 3. Admirals. 4. Women—Biography.] I. Title. II. Series.
    V63.H66M87 2004
    004'.092—dc22
    [B]

                                   2003026641

Printed in the United States of America

10 9 8 7 6 5 4 3 2 1

To Our Readers:
We have done our best to make sure all Internet Addresses in this book were active and appropriate when we
went to press. However, the author and the publisher have no control over and assume no liability for the material available on those Internet sites or on other Web sites they may link to. Any comments or suggestions can
be sent by e-mail to comments@enslow.com or to the address on the back cover.

Every effort has been made to locate all copyright holders of material used in this book. If any errors or omis-
sions have occurred, corrections will be made in future editions of this book.

Illustration Credits: © Bettmann/Corbis, p. 17L; Courtesy Unisys Corporation, pp. 22, 23, 25; Defense Visual
Information Center, p. 27; Grace Murray Hopper, pp. 6, 29; Grace Murray Hopper Collection, Archives Center,
National Museum of American History, Behring Center, Smithsonian Institution, p. 15; Harvard University
Archives, pp. 16, 17R; Library of Congress, p. 11; Mary Murray Wescote, pp. 7, 8–9, 12; Official U.S. Navy
photograph, from the collections of the Naval Historical Center, pp. 13, 18, 26, 28, 29; Photo courtesy of the
Computer History Museum, pp. 1, 20, 21, 29; Remington Rand, Co., p. 4; Special Collections, Vassar College
Libraries, p. 3.

Cover Illustration: Remington Rand, Co. (portrait). Spot art: Photos courtesy of the Computer History Museum.

Table of Contents

Grace Hopper

Chapter 1

"Amazing Grace"

Young Grace Murray liked to build things and take them apart. One day, Grace took apart an alarm clock, then another and another. How did a clock work? After seven alarm clocks, Grace's mother asked her to stop. But Grace was still curious. The more she learned, the more she wanted to know.

Grace Brewster Murray was born on December 9, 1906. It was a time of great change. Telephones, cars, and airplanes were new inventions. Grace, too, would become an inventor. Her work would change the world of computers and earn her the nickname "Amazing Grace."

Grace was the oldest child born to Walter and Mary Murray. She grew up in a happy home in New York City with a sister, Mary, and brother, Roger. The family spent summers in New Hampshire. Grace went boating and learned how to sew, cook, and garden.

From her mother, Grace learned to love math. From her father, she learned that anything

---

Grace was a busy, curious little girl.

Grace, left, with her father, sister Mary,
and baby brother Roger.

was possible. An illness had caused him to lose both of his legs. He told his children that if he could walk with wooden legs and canes, then they could do anything.

In those days, most girls did not go to college. But Grace's parents wanted her to get a good education

and follow her dreams. In 1924, Grace began her first year at Vassar College in Poughkeepsie, New York. She worked hard in school and helped her classmates study, too. She played basketball and other sports.

In 1928, Grace graduated from Vassar with top honors and a degree in math and physics. Next, she went on to study more math at Yale University in New Haven, Connecticut. She earned a master's degree in 1930. Grace's future was looking bright with the promise of a teaching job and a wedding.

Grace

Ten-year-old Grace with her classmates at the Graham School, a top private school in New York City.

Chapter 2

Becoming a Teacher

O n June 15, 1930, Grace married Vincent Foster Hopper. They had met one summer in New Hampshire. Both Vincent and Grace became teachers. Vincent taught English at New York University's School of Business. Grace taught math at Vassar College. Very few women were college math teachers at that time. Grace did a terrific job. She made math exciting to her students.

Grace was also learning even more about math at Yale University. In 1934, she earned a Ph.D., or doctorate—the highest university degree. Earning a Ph.D. in math was not easy. From 1934 to 1937, Yale awarded seven of these degrees. Only one went to a woman. That woman was Grace.

By 1941, Grace and Vincent were finding that their busy lives often kept them apart. Four years later, they divorced.

Across the ocean, in Europe, many countries were involved in World War II. The United States, Great Britain, China, and the Soviet Union were fighting against Germany, Italy, and Japan.

Yale is one of the best schools in the country. This famous Yale building is called Harkness Tower.

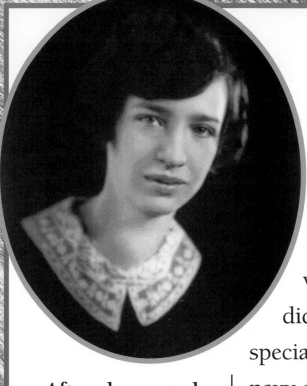

Grace, at age thirty-six, wanted to serve her country in the navy. In those days, women in the navy were called WAVES.

The navy told Grace she was too old to join. But Grace did not give up. She asked for special permission, and finally the navy agreed to let her in.

After she earned a Ph.D., Grace was called Dr. Hopper.

First, Grace was sent to the Midshipman's School for Women. There, she learned all about the navy and how to be a leader.

On June 27, 1944, Grace graduated at the top of her class and became a junior officer. She had no idea that her navy job would change her life.

This poster invited women to join the navy.

Share the Deeds of Victory

Join the WAVES

Chapter 3

Grace In the Navy

Grace was sent to work with navy officers at Harvard University in Cambridge, Massachusetts. Her talents in math would help run their computer, Mark I.

When Grace saw Mark I, her eyes grew bright. "I had to find out how it worked," she said. Mark I was like a giant calculator and could solve all kinds of math problems. It did three additions each second. Today, a computer can do trillions of additions every second. But Mark I was an amazing machine for its time.

To solve math problems, the computer needed a program—that is, a set of instructions to tell it what to do. The program was written in a computer code. This code was "punched" into paper tape, making a pattern of holes the computer could read. Then the tape was fed into Mark I. The computer read the tape and did its work.

Grace asked many questions. She wanted to learn everything about the giant computer.

Grace was proud to wear her navy uniform.

Because the country was at war, Grace and her team often worked all day and all night programming

Mark I was eight feet high and fifty-one feet long. It filled a huge room.

Mark I. Sometimes they did not go home for three days in a row. The navy needed Mark I to calculate where to aim its new guns and rockets.

Before long, Grace knew so much about Mark I that she could write a book. And so, she did. Her book taught others about Mark I and how to make it work.

Grace knew that each computer program was made up of many instructions in computer code. Together, they told the computer what to do. Often, some of the same computer-code instructions were used over and over again. Grace wrote these down in a notebook. Later, when she needed them again, she could copy the computer code from her notebook and type it into the hole-punching machine.

After the war, Grace stayed at Harvard. She loved working with computers. In 1946, she began using the bigger, faster Mark II and Mark III computers. One day, the Mark II computer shut down.

What was wrong? Inside the computer, Grace and her team found a moth.

Grace typed computer code on this keyboard, and the machine punched holes in the paper tape. Mark I could "read" the holes.

Problems with computers are nicknamed "bugs," and fixing them is called "debugging." Grace did not make up these terms, but she thought it was funny to find a *real* computer bug.

In 1949, Grace left Harvard to take a job with a computer company in Philadelphia, Pennsylvania. She was forty-three years old.

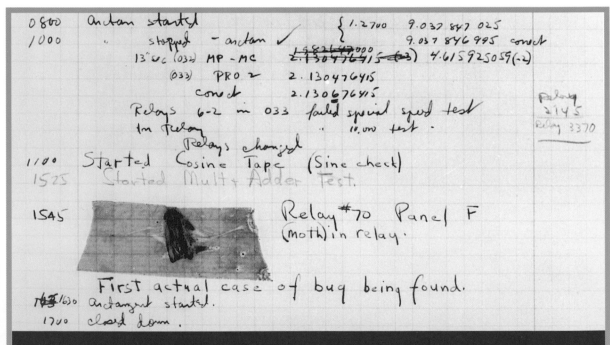

Grace saved the Mark II computer bug in her notebook.

Chapter 4

Computer Pioneer

Grace was well on her way to becoming a pioneer in the new world of computers. At the Eckert-Mauchly Computer Corporation, her first job was to get to know its BINAC (**Bin**ary **A**utomatic **C**omputer). The BINAC was the first electrical computer. It could store information and check its own work. Grace trained other people how to use the BINAC, too.

Next, Grace and her team began to program the

new UNIVAC I—the **Uni**versal **A**utomatic **C**omputer. UNIVAC I was a thousand times faster than Mark I and much smaller. Grace led her team in testing and improving the programming of UNIVAC I and, later, UNIVAC II.

Grace thought about ways to make computers easier for people to use. For every computer program, Grace had to type all the computer-code instructions onto the computer tape. She began to wonder.

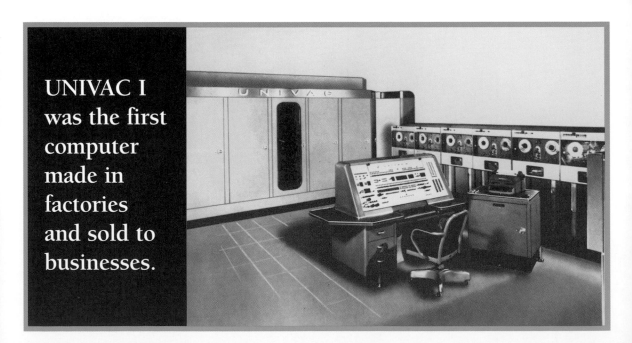

UNIVAC I was the first computer made in factories and sold to businesses.

Was it possible to make computers do some of this work?

Grace and her team started with the computer code in her notebook. Each set of instructions was recorded on magnetic tape, fed into the computer, and given a nickname. Now the code was stored in the computer. When Grace typed a nickname, the computer read that set of instructions. When Grace typed many nicknames in a row, the computer read all those sets of instructions in order.

UNIVAC I ran on magnetic metal tape, not paper tape.

Grace and her team were on to something big. They had invented the first computer compiler.

Soon after, they had another important idea. Writing computer code was hard for many people. Could computer programs use English words instead

Grace knew that the COBOL computer language would help businesses.

of computer code? Grace and her team wrote a computer language called Flowmatic. It used commands like COUNT, DIVIDE, and MOVE.

In 1959, Grace was asked to join a group of companies and the U.S. Department of Defense to help create a common business language. In those days, three different computer languages were being used by companies in the United States. They were IBM Fortran, Automatically Programmed Tools, and Flowmatic.

It would be better if businesses all used the same computer language.

To make this happen, the group developed COBOL (**C**ommon **B**usiness **O**riented **L**anguage). It soon became the most popular computer language.

Grace was not the inventor of COBOL, but she planted its seeds and helped it grow. She convinced many companies that using COBOL was a good idea. That is why she is often called the Mother of COBOL.

Grace had ideas to make the UNIVAC
work better and faster.

Chapter 5

Teaching Others

I n 1966, when she was sixty years old, Grace received a letter from the navy. It was time for her to retire—to stop working. Grace loved her work, and she said that retiring was "the saddest day of my life." But just one year later, in 1967, the navy needed Grace's help again.

The navy asked Grace to do more work on their computer programs. They also asked her to teach

Grace taught many people how to program computers.

navy officers how to use COBOL and to write a navy COBOL instruction book. Grace said, "Yes!"

For the next nineteen years, Grace worked for the navy. She traveled around the country speaking to navy officers about COBOL. She also wrote many articles and reports about computer language. She helped write a textbook about computers, and she gave speeches at colleges and companies about the future of computers.

Grace believed that someday, many people would have their own computers. She said that some of these computers would be small enough to fit into people's hands. Many of Grace's ideas have come true.

Over the years, Grace won many awards and honors for her work. In 1984, she was the first woman to be named a navy rear admiral. That is one of the highest titles for a navy officer. On August 14, 1986, Grace retired from the navy for the last time. The navy honored her in a ceremony aboard the USS *Constitution*.

Commander Joseph Brown thanked Grace for her 43 years in the navy.

Grace was seventy-nine years old. Still, she did not stop working. She joined the Digital Equipment Company. Once again, Grace began traveling to talk to people about computers. In the last years of her life, Grace became famous. Television stations, newspapers, and magazines asked her to talk about computers.

On January 1, 1992, Grace died at age eighty-five. She was buried with full military honors at Arlington National Cemetery. In 1995, a navy warship, the USS *Hopper*, was named after her.

USS *Hopper*

Some people say that Grace's greatest works were the compiler and COBOL. But Grace did not agree.

Grace helped lead the way into the world of computers.

She often said that her greatest gift was serving her country in the navy. And she believed that her greatest work was teaching young people. She called them "our future."

Grace was famous for telling her students not to listen when anyone said, "We've always done it this way!" In Grace's office, she had a clock with hands that ran backward. The clock showed that there is always more than one way to do anything. Grace Hopper's life was proof of that.

Timeline

1906~Born on December 9 in New York City.

1928~Graduates from Vassar College.

1934~Earns Ph.D. in math from Yale University.

1944~Graduates from the U.S. Navy's Midshipman School. Begins work on Mark I at Harvard University.

1949~Works with BINAC and UNIVAC I at the Eckert-Mauchly Corporation.

1952~Develops first computer compiler.

1957~Develops Flowmatic computer language, –1960 then helps develop COBOL.

1985~Becomes a navy rear admiral.

1986~Retires from the navy; joins Digital Equipment Company.

1992~Dies January 1 at home in Arlington, Virginia.

Words to Know

compiler—A computer program that takes the programmer's nickname for a set of instructions and changes it into computer code that the computer can read.

magnetic tape—Tape coated with a magnetic material on which information can be stored.

physics—The science that studies matter and energy. Everything in the world is made up of matter.

program—Instructions telling a computer what to do.

programmer—The person who writes a computer program.

retire—To give up working at a job.

WAVES—**W**omen **A**ccepted for **V**olunteer **E**mergency **S**ervice. This name for women in the navy was used from 1942 to 1948.

World War II—A war fought in Europe from 1939 to 1945, with countries from Europe, Asia, and North America.

Learn More

Books

Drake, Jim. *What Is a Computer?* Chicago, Ill.: Heinemann Library, 1999.

Mattern, Joanne. *Grace Hopper: Computer Pioneer.* New York: PowerKids Press, 2003.

Whitelaw, Nancy. *Grace Hopper: Programming Pioneer.* New York: Scientific American Books for Young Readers, 1995.

Internet Addresses

Grace Murray Hopper: Pioneer Computer Scientist <http://www.sdsc.edu/ScienceWomen/hopper.html>

Grace Murray Hopper <http://www.cs.yale.edu/homes/tap/Files/hopper-story.html>

WIC Biography: Grace Hopper <http://www.wic.org/bio/ghopper.htm>

Index